I-SPY

with David Bellamy

DINOSAURS

I-Spy Books
12 Star Road, Partridge Green
Horsham, Sussex RH13 8RA

'I-Spy Dinosaurs?—impossible', you may say, 'they all became extinct 65 million years ago'. And, of course, you would be right. But that doesn't mean that we can't see things which relate to them and their time-span.

So let's go to work, the serious work of discovering dinosaurs on an egg. No points for spying an egg, but as you dissect one for breakfast, see how many layers you can see.

SCORING

As you spot each of the dinosaurs here—and answer the simple question—you can earn an I-SPY score. When your scores total 1250 you may award yourself the rank of DINOSAUROLOGIST with Silver Honours. When they reach a complete total of 1500 points you are entitled to the rank of DINOSAUROLOGIST with Gold Honours; you may then send your book to me, and I shall return it to you stamped with my personal seal. Your certificate of rank is on the inside-back-cover of this book.
Good hunting!

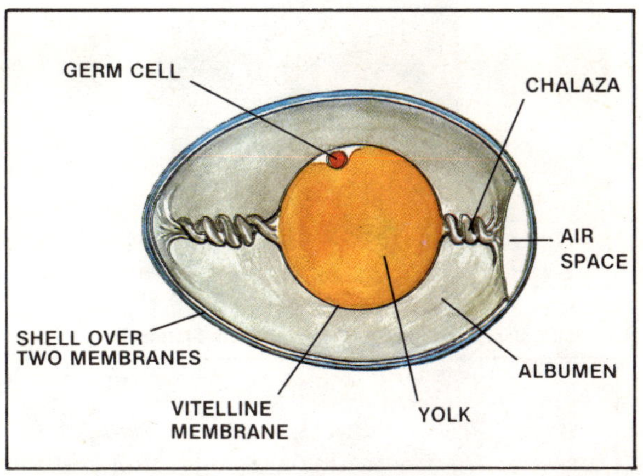

Dinosaurs were reptiles which, like the modern birds, laid eggs. The tough but porous shell protects the egg, allowing it to breathe. The albumen (it's not white until you cook it) provides water, and the yolk a food supply for the developing embryo. The egg cell proper is inside the CHORION, and the AMNION (unfortunately you won't be able to see these in a cooked egg) encloses a fluid-filled chamber, inside which the embryo can develop safe in its own private pool of water, despite the fact that it is laid on dry land.

It was the shelled egg with all its layers which gave the reptiles the freedom of the dry land which they ruled for 140 million years. That means that the first dinosaurs were tramping about on the earth around 200 million years ago. A long time, but it is easy to see something which is much older than that! What?
Here are some clues.

Lea Hall Colliery and Rugeley Power Station, Staffordshire.

Dump-truck and other machines at work on an opencast coalmine site.

The restoration, by the National Coal Board's Opencast Executive, of more than 400 acres of formerly derelict land after the extraction of 1.5 million tonnes of coal: Shipley Park, Derbyshire.

Digging the pit and excavating the coal produces lots of waste. This is usually piled up in the form of gigantic pit heaps. In the old days they were very unsightly, but today most are kept neat and tidy, and when the pits have come to the end of their working life they are landscaped and planted with grass or trees.

In certain areas where the deposits are not too far underground, coal is mined by opencasting. Giant drag-lines and dumper trucks (some as big as dinosaurs!) are used to remove the overburden and expose rich seams.

The N.C.B. are experts and they can do an excellent job getting it out and rehabilitating the land.

N.C.B.—National Coal Board. Yes, the product in question is coal, the bulk of which was laid down during the CARBONIFEROUS PERIOD, that is between 280 and 345 million years ago, long before any dinosaur lived. When I was at school, coal was in common use and it produced an awful lot of smoke and soot. For health reasons its use is now banned in many areas and we use smokeless fuel instead.

Do you have your own museum at home? If so, it should contain a piece of coal—an object three hundred million years old!

"COME ON, YOU CAN'T PUT IT OFF FOR EVER, I WANT TO SEE A REAL DINOSAUR!"
—And so do I. So it's off to the museum. However, on the way you may be getting closer to dinosaurs all the time . . .

BANK OF ENGLAND

"WHAT'S THAT GOT TO DO WITH DINOSAURS?"
Well, for a start, the manager would like a couple to help him guard the money and, for a finish (and what a finish) it's made of PORTLAND STONE. A lovely white stone ideal for building banks and other important buildings and, you've guessed it, it was laid down during dinosaur times. It gets its name from Portland in Dorset, which is good dinosaur country—or at least it was when the PORTLAND STONE and the overlying PURBECK BEDS were being laid down.

To prove it, many of the quarries are rich sources of dinosaur remains and gigantic footprints, casts of which will be found in many museums.

Draw your own tracks to scale beside them.

Above, Megalosaurus tracks from Dorset, re-sited outside the Natural History Museum, South Kensington.

In which museum did you see dinosaur footprints?........
............Score **20**

AMMONITE FOSSIL

AMMONITE

Some of the commonest fossils you will find in a museum, and even in peoples' gardens, are AMMONITES. They are the shells, up to nearly 2 metres across, of gigantic octopus-like creatures which lived in the sea, some at the same time as the dinosaurs. I often wonder what happened if a dinosaur stood on an ammonite—were their shells dinosaur-proof?

In which museum did you see an ammonite?......................

.... Score **15**

Now you are inside the museum (and you may well have to visit a number of different ones, but that won't worry you, because they are such super places), we can get down to the real McCoy. What is more, as you can't expect every museum to have a complete collection of reconstructions of dinosaurs, points can be scored for actual skeletons or casts of the whole, or parts of the animals, or for models (and some are life-size), or for pictures in museum dioramas.

. . . So let's start with the biggest.

SUPERSAURUS

—Well, that's what Reader's Digest called it when it was discovered in 1972, and the scientists haven't yet given it an official name so that will do for us.

15 metres tall, at least 30 metres long, and weighing over 80 tonnes. Unless you go to America the likelihood of seeing any part of this monster is pretty remote. So, to gain points, go into the garden or park and visualize just how vast this animal must have been.

First, pace out its 30 metres length on the ground. It's easiest to estimate its height against a tree or a building, so, find a friend who is 1.5 metres tall, or a stick of that height, stand him or her (or it) against the tree and walk back until, holding a ruler at arm's length, your friend (or the pole) measures 2 cms against the ruler. Now measure ten times that height up the ruler and sight that point against the tree. That's how high Supersaurus would be if he were standing there!

Now draw to scale what you *think it looked like, and*
....Score **30**

MOUSE AND MUSSAURUS PATAGONICUS AND ITS EGG

The majority of dinosaurs were not great lumbering giants. In fact many were small, and the smallest found to date was about the size of a thrush! It was only found very recently in Argentina and the scientists have only just chosen its official name. What would you have called it?

Well, they called it *Mussaurus patagonicus*—the Mouse Dinosaur from Patagonia.

This is another dinosaur that you probably won't be able to find evidence of, so score for seeing a thrush (or a mouse!)

Score **25**

You will probably spy yours with its feathers on, but as we shall see later there is much more linking the dinosaurs to the birds than just the eggs, and it's all to do with their skeletons.

SKELETON OF THRUSH

And while you are on the trail of a thrush, how about its egg? No, **don't** disturb the nest, wait until the chicks have hatched and collect the pieces of shell, put them together and measure the length. And if you haven't any thrushes near you, but only blackbirds, that's OK because blackbirds are thrushes too.

*The length of my..egg was..*Score 25

The egg of the smallest dinosaur was only 25mm long—I wonder what colour it was.

The largest dinosaur could have been around 40 metres long and have weighed 200 tonnes. If this is proved, it would make it bigger than the largest Blue Whale.

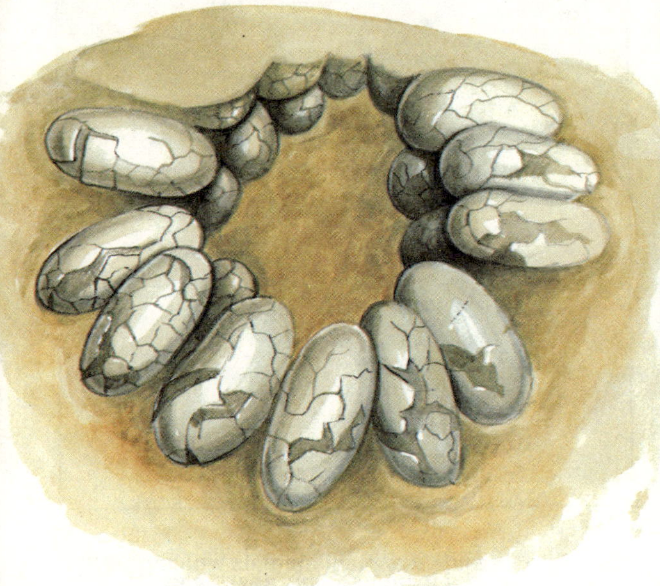

NEST OF DINOSAUR EGGS

DINOSAURS' EGGS

For any eggs, models or pictures of eggs in the museum, award yourself the marks.

I saw my eggs at...Score **30**

FEMALE OSTRICH SETTLING DOWN ON EGGS

You might imagine that giant animals would produce giant eggs. This is not the case and, if you have a think about it, you will see why. A giant egg would have to have a giant shell, so thick that the embryo would be unable to get sufficient oxygen. And how would the baby dinosaur ever break out? The largest of the eggs we know are about 25cm long, small enough to do their vital job with complete efficiency.

Where did you see an ostrich egg! ....Score **25**

PTERODACTYL

The flying reptiles were a group which not only included *Pterodactylus* but also *Pteranodon*, which had a large, long fin on its head. This may have helped in steering whilst in flight, or as a wind-operated counterbalance when catching a large fish from the surface of the water when in flight. By the way, *Pterodactylus* and *Pteranodon* are not, or were not, dinosaurs. They belonged to a separate group of prehistoric reptiles, the *Pterosaurs*.

I saw my Pterodactylus at..Score 25

I saw my Pteranodon at..Score **25**

The nearest thing we will ever see to a *Pterosaur* (pronounce it 'terro sore') in flight is a bat. But bats are mammals and are mainly insect eaters.

BAT

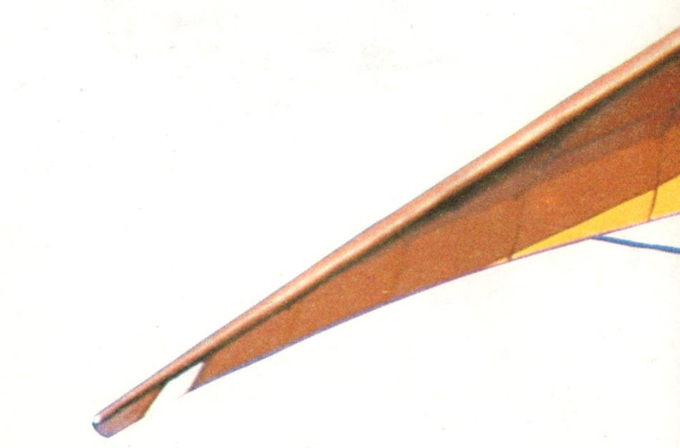

Where I saw one..
When I saw it.. Score **40**

Hang gliders also bear some resemblance, despite the fact that their wings do not flap. Make a drawing comparing the wing structures of all three; better still, make a series of paper cut-outs.

HANG GLIDER

Where I saw a hang glider..Score **40**

Sir Richard Owen first coined the name Dinosaur in 1841—it means terrible lizard.

DINOSAUR SKULLS

So what exactly is a dinosaur?
    Well, starting at the top, all dinosaurs have **diapsid** skulls, and diapsid skulls have two pairs of openings.

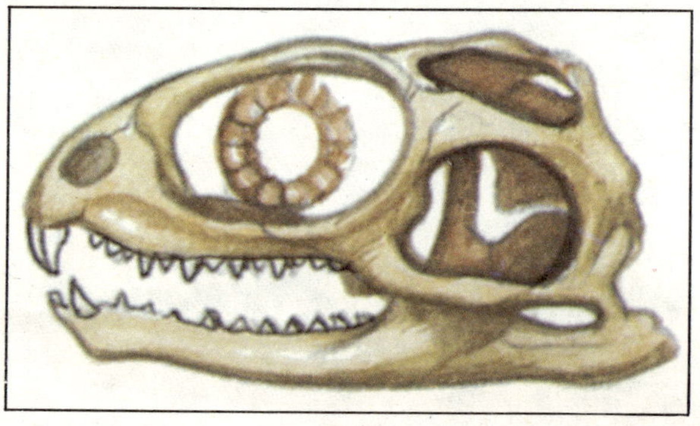

DIAPSID SKULL

Modern snakes, lizards and crocodiles have diapsid skulls, so it shouldn't be too difficult to find one at the museum or zoo.

Where I saw my diapsid skull..Score **35**

But what distinguishes true dinosaurs? The answer is, ALL DINOSAURS WALK WELL. Their limbs support the body from beneath, holding it clear above the ground. Going walkies? (. . . there's a good boy).

Above, a newt in water. On dry land a newt is a sprawler; its body lies on the ground, its legs stick out sideways and it hurries along with an 'S' shaped motion.

Where you saw one ....Score **35**

A crocodile or alligator, when it comes to walking, is a semi-improved animal. A crocodile in a hurry lifts its body clear off the ground—WATCH OUT!

Where you saw one ....Score **40**

Now watch a dog walk—a dachshund is ideal. The limbs support the body from underneath and, unless its owner is giving it too much to eat, not even its tummy drags on the ground. Like the dinosaurs. When it comes to going walkies, even slowly, dogs are FULLY IMPROVED ANIMALS.

So: dinosaurs were fully improved walkers with diapsid skulls. Now we're getting somewhere, as did the dinosaurs—for 140 million years!

DON'T CHICKEN OUT—THERE'S STILL LOTS MORE TO SEE!

SACRAL SKELETON OF A CHICKEN

Where did you eat chicken? ....

What did you do with the wishbone? ....

You have wished on the wishbone, which is part of what? ....

Now you are holding the pelvic or hip girdle in your greasy fingers, to which were attached two strong legs.

There were two main lines of dinosaurs: those with lizard-like hips, and those with bird-like hips.

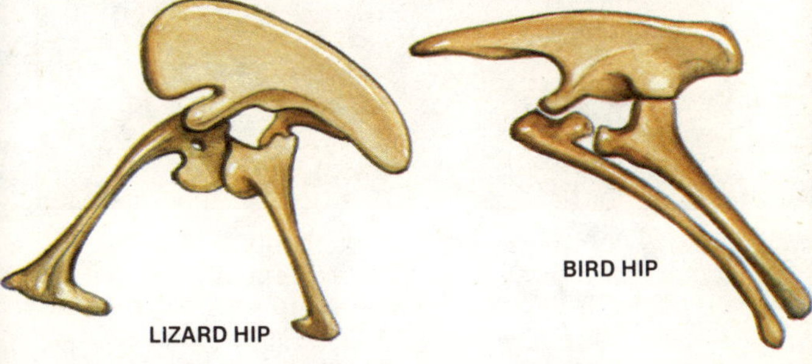

Note the difference and colour the bones which you think are common to those on the chicken hips.

You are now entering the world of anatomic homology. Award yourself 40 points and wash your fingers!

Meanwhile, back in the museum . . .

ALLOSAURUS (meaning 'different lizard')

It was 10 metres long and 4 metres tall, was a carnivore and closely related to, though larger than, the *Megalosaurus*—the animal which left its foot-prints all over southern England. It walked on its enormous three-toed back legs, and is a member of the group of lizard hips. *Allosaurus* is related to the terrible *Tyrannosaurus rex,* but more of him later.

Allosaurus: Where and what did you see? ....

....Score **45**

Sauropodomorpha (go on, try and say it) included the gigantic, four-footed plant-eating dinosaurs, like my favourite, Brontosaurus ('will you wait for me!').

Opposite, two Sauropods: tall *Brachiosaurus* in the foreground and long *Diplodocus* in the background.

DIPLODOCUS

Please note the spelling, and don't fall into the trap of saying Diplodotus. The name means 'double beam' and, with that long neck and tail, and vast bulk to support, it is aptly named.

For a long time *Diplodocus* and its four-footed, vegetable-eating relatives were thought to live in swamps. The argument was that the buoyancy of the water would help to support much of their weight. However, everything about them points away from that conclusion, especially the length of the neck. At first sight it seems perfect, a long snorkel, but the problem would be that the chest muscles, even of a dinosaur, would be unable to work that deep under water—the pressure would be too great.

There was no need for watery support; that fully improved locomotion was sufficient to raise the giant bodies clear off the ground.

Diplodocus was also a Lizard Hip.

Diplodocus: Where and what did you see? ....
....Score **40**

When you get there, don't miss the *Diplodocus*. It is the most amazing sight. Then walk through into the Whale Hall, and see the life-size model of the biggest animal that has ever lived **and still lives** — the Blue Whale. Not a dinosaur, but a mammal like you and me.

IGUANODON

One of the bird hipped dinosaurs—9 metres long, 5 metres tall and weighing about 4½ tonnes. It was a herbivore, and left its footprints along with *Megalosaurus*, which probably preyed on it. From its footprints there is little doubt that it walked in the main on its large back legs. However the smaller front feet are in part covered with a hoof, suggesting that at least sometimes it used its front feet for walking, and there are footprints to prove it.

Where did you see it?..

What did you see?..Score **45**

29

Dinosaur teeth were first discovered and recognised as something very special by Dr. and Mrs. Algernon Mantell in Sussex in 1822.

DINOSAUR FOOD

Both *Iguanodon* and *Diplodocus* were herbivores, which meant that they always ate up their vegetables. We know this by the shape of their teeth. To introduce dinosaur teeth, there is nothing better than a little animal, the skeleton of which has been found in South Africa. It was given the name *Hetero* (different) *Donto* (toothed) *Saurus* (lizard)—*HETERODONTOSAURUS.*

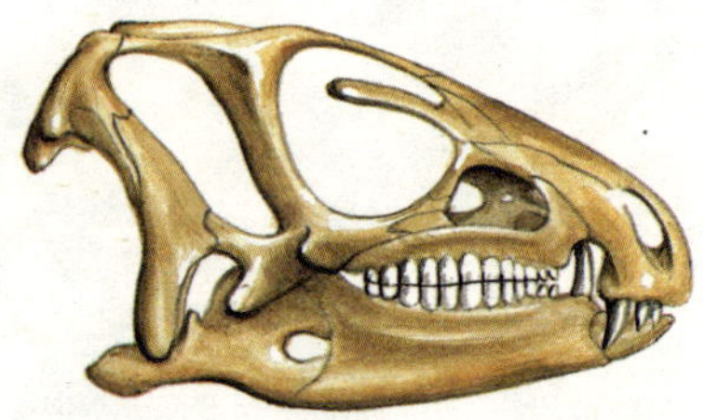

SKULL OF HETERODONTOSAURUS

A very descriptive name—just look at its teeth. At the front, simple teeth at the top which worked against a toothless beak at the bottom, ideal for ripping off branches and leaves. At the back, a wonderful set of tall teeth arranged very close together and worn down to give a long flat chewing surface. What is more, the surface of these teeth was ridged and grooved so that they worked rather like a pair of crimping scissors; ideal for chewing up the tough plant material ready for digestion.

But look at the large, curved teeth in between; they look very much like the canine teeth of a flesh-eating dog. Well, we don't know what *Heterodontosaurus* used these for—perhaps to snarl at other Heterodontosauruses who tried to pinch their lunch!

CARNIVORE & HERBIVORE

A CANINE AND FLESH-
   TEARING TEETH

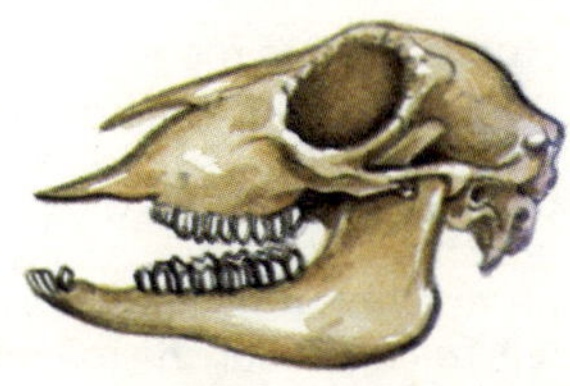

B CHEWING, GRINDING
   PLANT-EATING TEETH

A. *On what animal did you see them?* ....
....Score **40**

B. *On what animal did you see them?* ....
....Score **40**

HORSETAILS

In many gardens these are a weedy nuisance, for once they have got a roothold they are very difficult to get rid of.

FERTILE CONES OF COMMON HORSETAIL

Horsetails are members of the great Horsetail clan of plants which have lived on earth for more than 350 million years. In the past many were giant, tree-like plants, the remains of which helped to form coal and later feed the dinosaurs. Feel the texture of your garden horsetail. It is very rough to the touch, because it is full of silica, one reason why they fossilize so well. Another country name for horsetails is Scouring Rushes, because they do make excellent pan scrubbers (NOT on non-stick pans, though, or your Mum will descend on you and me like a ton of Supersaurus!). The silica must have worn the chewing teeth away very rapidly, and I should think a *Diplodocus* with toothache was not a pretty sight—or sound!

Where did you see your Horsetail fossil?..............................

....Score **40**

CYCADS

Despite the fact that the horsetails have cones, they are more closely related to the ferns than to the true cone-bearers. At about the time that the dinosaurs were noisily going about their many ways of life across the earth, the cone-bearing plants were quietly doing the same. The cycads have a long history and the ancestors of the modern ones, which live in the tropics and are grown in conservatories and even in up-market restaurants and offices, certainly fed the dinosaurs.

MALE CONES OF WHITE-HAIRED CYCAD

Where did you see your Cycad? ....
What sort was it? ....
Did it have a cone? .... Score **40**

Feel the texture of the leaves and the cone—no wonder the dinosaurs needed efficient teeth to deal with that lot.

GINKGO

Another dinosaur snack plant—this beautiful tree is grown in many of our parks and the gardens of stately homes. It has an interesting history for, though known from various parts of the earth as a fossil, it was only found growing in Chinese temple gardens, a relict from the past.

More recently, it has been found growing in the wild, again in China. Its soft leaves which look not unlike those of a Maidenhair Fern (hence its other name, the Maidenhair Tree), and its juicy yellow fruits, must have made a welcome change from eating horsetails and cycads.

MAIDENHAIR FERN

Where did you see it?..Score **30**

I saw my first one in my Auntie's sitting room.

MAIDENHAIR TREE

Where did you see it?..Score **40**

I saw my first one in the grounds of the Baptist Church in Sutton, Surrey.

DINOSAUR DROPPINGS

With all that tough leaf material, you can guess that
the plant-eaters had some difficulty in digesting their
food. The scientific name for ancient dung or spoor
droppings is Coprolites and, though you may think
that it must be a rather distasteful occupation to be a
coproliteologist, we can learn a lot about the animals
from their study.

DINOSAUR DROPPING—COPROLITE

Where did you see yours?..Score **50**

If there is a Loch Ness Monster, it isn't a dinosaur; much more likely a paddle-limbed Plesiosaur.

DUCK-BILLED DINOSAURS

No, no relation to the Duck-billed Platypus, which is a mammal, although its ancestors were living at the same time.

These were Bird-hipped forms which probably walked on all fours for much of the time. They had a broad, flat tail and webbed fingers, which suggests that they spent some of their lives in water.

DUCK-BILLED DINOSAUR

What did you see?...

What sort?...

Where?...Score **55**

What did you see?..
What sort?...
Where?...Score **60**

As the palaeontologists (people who study prehistoric animals) find more and more remains, their ideas about these animals change. What do you think the crests were for?

....

The teeth of the duck-bills are of great interest too—hundreds of small grinding teeth in rows at the back of the jaws, suggesting tough food.

TYRANNOSAURUS REX

If you had actually seen one of these, you would probably not have lived to tell the tale—they were very active predators!

This incredible animal was 5 metres tall, 13 metres long, weighing 8 tonnes, with serrated teeth 15 cm long. It must have run on its giant hind legs with a rather waddling gait, for its footprints are found one behind the other. Speeds? Well, it has been estimated that *Triceratops,* on which it fed, could top 48 kilometres an hour—fantastic; like a runaway tank! I wonder what it was really like back in the dinosaur days, and I wonder, if man had lived then, whether we could, with our superior mammalian brains, have outwitted these monsters and their diminutive kin.

What did you see of Tyrannosaurus rex?..

Where did you see it?...Score **60**

TRICERATOPS—THREE-HORNED FACE

With the Tyrant Lizards on the rampage, it is no wonder that many of the other animals had to have efficient mechanisms of defence and protection. The best known are the Horned Dinosaurs, mainly because *Triceratops* have been drawn, painted and modelled many times. They were very common in North America at the end of the dinosaur era 65 to 70 million years ago. Then, great herds roamed the plains of that great continent, feeding on a wealth of cone- and flower-bearing plants.

7 metres long and weighing 7 tonnes, three vicious horns and thick leathery skin, together with the herding instinct, made them worthy opponents for *Tyrannosaurus* himself, or herself—the females were just as ferocious.

TRICERATOPS

Another Horned Dinosaur, *Styracosaurus*, is on the back cover.

What did you see of a horned dinosaur?......................................

What sort was it?......................................

Where did you see it?......................................Score **55**

THE PLATED DINOSAURS

STEGOSAURUS — THE ROOF LIZARD

Perhaps the most famous of the plated giants. 9 metres long, weighing almost 2 tonnes, its tail carried spines and its back, which was arched because its back legs were longer than its front ones, was furnished with large, sail-like plates, the largest being over its Bird Hips.

STEGOSAURUS

KENTROSAURUS

What did you see and where? ....

.... Score **55**

There is much discussion concerning the function of the plates, but none concerning the protective function of the four tail spikes. The plates, which made the animal look much bigger than it actually was, were well supplied with blood, so may well have had a heat regulating function, like the ears of elephants.

Kentrosaurus was sort of a half way house, with spines at the back and plates at the front.

What did you see of Kentrosaurus and where?......................

....Score **60**

THE ARMOURED DINOSAURS

The Plated Dinosaurs, though immensely successful, died out around 140 million years ago. Their place was taken by another group, the Ankylosaurs, which were to become just as successful.

POLACANTHUS

My favourite is *Polacanthus,* which lived on the Isle of Wight around 115 million years ago (before it was an isle and before there was an English Channel). I like this one because I helped an amateur dinosaurologist by the name of Bill Blows to excavate one on the beach. Bill Blows has been studying dinosaurs on the Isle of Wight since he was six years old. It's never too young to start!

What did you see of which Armoured Dinosaur, and where?..Score **60**

There's always something going on in the world of dinosaur research. Either something just dug up, or a scientist with new ideas about how they lived. In Britain two important fossil discoveries in 1983 made headlines—a new carnivore in Surrey and an Iguanodon's skull on the Isle of Wight. But not everything gets into the papers. Ask at your museum what's new!

ANKYLOSAURUS

Ankylosaurus—Stiff Lizard, was just that. 4.5 metres long with a broad, blunt head. The whole of its back was covered in thick yet flexible armour—bony plates set in a leathery skin. A row of short, sharp spikes along its flanks and a big bony club on the end of its tail. Not an easy mouthful for any would-be predator.

What did you see of Ankylosaurus and where?................

.... Score **60**

The ancestors of our crocodiles, tortoises and turtles, and snakes evolved during the time of the dinosaurs, but managed to survive though dinosaurs died out.

MONKEY PUZZLES AND MAGNOLIAS

The dinosaurs came, evolved to fill the many roles open to them in their prehistoric world, held their own massive and very successful sway, and then became extinct. They disappeared off the face of the earth, and not even the most expert of experts really knows why.

They left the living world a very different place—their place taken by the birds and mammals, and, some 64 million years later, by man.

MONKEY PUZZLE TREE
(Araucaria)

It might puzzle a monkey to make its home in an *Araucaria*, but I don't think it would puzzle a dinosaur to eat it. *Araucaria* is one of the cone bearers. Its ancestors were once widespread across the world. Now, it and its relatives are restricted in nature to the Southern Hemisphere, although the Monkey Puzzle can be seen growing in many suburban gardens. It became popular in gardens in Victorian times and, indeed, was a status symbol before the days of motor cars.

Where did you see a Monkey Puzzle?...

Was it in cone?..Score **35**

MAGNOLIA

It was during the reign of the dinosaurs that the first flower-bearing plants grew on earth, around 130 million years ago, gradually becoming a more and more important part of the vegetation on which birds perch and animals feed. The first flowering plants were woody, and they had simple flowers consisting of whorls of separate sepals and petals, all of which were modified leaves, lots of anthers bearing the pollen sacs full of pollen, and lots of separate carpels holding and protecting the egg and the embryo as it developed inside the seed. If the layered egg was one of the reasons for the success of the dinosaurs living on land, the seed spelt the same story of success for the land plants, the cone- and the flower-bearers.

Where did you see a Magnolia, and what colour were the flowers?...Score **35**

There were hundreds of different sorts of dinosaurs; we don't know how many, but we do know they all became extinct. There are more than 250,000 sorts of flower-bearing plants living today, many of which may become extinct in the not too distant future. And we won't be able to blame the dinosaurs.

JOIN THE I-SPY CLUB

- All you need to join the I-SPY Club is to buy a Membership Book which includes the secret codes. Ask at your bookshop or newsagent.

- Tell your friends about I-SPY. Invite them to join and form a Patrol with you.

- Collect all the I-SPY books—and you'll have a wonderful library of your own.

- Write to me about any interesting discoveries you make. You may win a prize! Remember to enclose a stamped addressed envelope for a reply.

LOOK OUT FOR THESE I-SPY WITH DAVID BELLAMY BOOKS

AT THE AIRPORT	ON A CAR JOURNEY
ARCHAEOLOGY	CAR NUMBERS
AT THE ART GALLERY	CARS
BIRDS AND REPTILES AT THE ZOO	CIVIL AIRCRAFT
	GARDEN BIRDS
BRITISH COINS	TREES

AND MANY MORE! TO COME

A PIGEON

Of all the animals I have ever met, I reckon that the good old common, or back garden, pigeon takes me closest to the dinosaurs, because some of the experts believe that our modern birds are descendants of the Bird-hipped line of dinosaurs.

Where did you see your pigeon? ....Score **15**

Make a comparison between what you now know about dinosaurs and what you know about birds, and then go to the museum and look for *Archaeopteryx*. It is the oldest known fossil bird, dating from around 100 million years ago, and still had many reptilian characteristics, including teeth and a long bony tail.

ARCHAEOPTERYX

Where did you see it?.............

....

Score **65**

It also had feathers. I agree with some of the experts that our modern birds are, in fact, flying dinosaurs. How about you?

INDEX

I-Spy are grateful to Jenny Halstead for the artwork, and for photographs to the Bank of England, Heather Angel, Animal Photography, National Coal Board, Steve Thompson, Yorkshire TV, and 'Shell Times' for David Bellamy on p.2. Series Editor, Anthony Maynard.

Published by Ravette Limited, 12 Star Road, Partridge Green, Horsham, West Sussex RH13 8RA © Ravette Ltd. 1983. Printed in Italy (KEL)
ISBN 0-906710-32-4